Therefore go and make disciples of all nations, baptizing them in the name of the Father and of the Son and of the Holy Spirit, and teaching them to obey everything I have commanded you. And surely I am with you always, to the very end of the age.

Matthew 28:19-20 (NIV)

potential ideas
- tutoring / homework help / read aloud
- taxes & tacos
  do your own with each other's help
  (not tax experts)

EXPANDING THE EXPEDITION REACH

With Missional Communities

Rachel Gilmore

EXPANDING THE EXPEDITION REACH

With Missional Communities

©2021 Rachel Gilmore

books@marketsquarebooks.com
P.O. Box 23664 Knoxville, Tennessee 37933
ISBN: 978-1-950899-26-5

Printed and Bound in the United States of America
Cover Illustration & Book Design ©2021 Market Square Publishing, LLC
Editors: Kristin Lighter and Kay Kotan

Scripture quotations are from

(NIV)
THE HOLY BIBLE, NEW INTERNATIONAL VERSION®, NIV®
Copyright © 1973, 1978, 1984, 2011 by Biblica, Inc.® Used by permission.
All rights reserved worldwide.

This resource was commissioned as
one of many interconnected steps in the
journey of *The Greatest Expedition*.

the greatest
EXPEDITION

GreatestExpedition.com

Table of Contents

assumed "givens" that I struggle with:
  prayer - p. 7-8
  baptism - p. 16

Foreword

This resource was commissioned as one of many interconnected steps in the journey of *The Greatest Expedition*. While each step is important individually, we intentionally built the multi-step Essentials Pack and the Expansion Pack to provide a richer and fuller experience with the greatest potential for transformation and introducing more people to a relationship with Jesus Christ. For more information, visit GreatestExpedition.org.

However, we also recognize you may be exploring this resource apart from *The Greatest Expedition*. You might find yourself on a personal journey, a small group journey, or perhaps a church leadership team journey.

We are so glad you are on this journey!

As you take each step in your expedition, your Expedition Team will discover whether the ministry tools you will be exploring will be utilized only for the Expedition Team or if this expedition will be a congregational journey. Our hope and prayer is *The Greatest Expedition* is indeed a congregational journey, but if it proves to be a solo journey for just the Expedition Team, God will still do amazing things through your intentional exploration, discernment, and faithful next steps.

Regardless of how you came to discover *The Greatest Expedition,* it will pave the way to a new God-inspired expedition. Be brave and courageous on your journey through *The Greatest Expedition!*

Kay L Kotan, PCC
Director, *The Greatest Expedition*

CHAPTER ONE

What is a Missional Community?

In April of 2016, while I was in England with a group of church planters on a study tour, I heard about a movement that has changed my life. I met Graham Horsley, the Connexional Fresh Expressions Missioner for the Methodist Church, who talked about being a part of the Fresh Expressions movement that was revitalizing the kingdom of God throughout the United Kingdom. I had never heard of Fresh Expressions, and as I met their lay and clergy leaders and heard words like "Messy Church" and "Dinner Church," I was hooked!

I came home and started applying what I had learned in England to my own church plant in Virginia Beach. It didn't take long before I realized that there were fresh expressions within driving distance of my church. I went to visit a "Messy Church" connected to Williamsburg United Methodist Church where up to 100 people gather once a month for a meal and family-friendly, "hands-on" worship service. I brought my kids with me to see what this type of fresh expression was all about and when they walked into the space and saw the bounce house and Lego table, they were hooked, too! We had a fun night exploring Scripture together as a family through a variety of activities and songs. That night had a meaningful impact on my family and we launched our own Messy Church[1] two months later.

Travis Collins wrote a book called *Fresh Expressions of Church*[2] where he defines a fresh expression as, "a new form of church for

---

[1] https://messychurchusa.org.

[2] Collins, Travis, Fresh Expressions of Church, Seedbed Publishing, 2015.

the new world in which we live." He goes on to share the definition offered by the Church of England and the British Methodist Church in 2006:

> *A fresh expression is a form of church for our changing culture established primarily for the benefit of people who are not yet members of any church. It will come into being through principles of listening, service, incarnational mission and making disciples. It will have the potential to become a mature expression of church shaped by the gospel and the enduring marks of the church and for its cultural context.*

So why am I using the term *missional community,* and how does that differ from the term *fresh expression?* While the two terms are used interchangeably, both in the United States and Great Britain, the term "missional community" emphasizes the relational nature of the faith community. There's a purpose, a *mission* that drives and energizes this gathering of people.

When I'm asked to define a "missional

community" to those inside or outside of the church, I've found that the easiest definition is, *"a missional community is new faces in new spaces."* It's really that simple. It's about forming relationships with people outside of your church who are not likely to ever walk into the church building.

I once worked with a gifted worship leader who also served as a "theologian-in-residence" at the church. He would regularly remind us of the William Temple quote, "The church is the only institution that exists primarily for the benefit of those who are not its members." While that quote should be true in every church, it is most definitely the case in a missional community!

So you are not starting a missional community if you add a young adult Sunday School class to your Sunday morning programming schedule. You are not starting a missional community if your "Nifty over Fifty" Men's group decides to meet at iHop on Wednesday mornings for the early bird special and plan their next outreach event. You are starting a missional community if you meet virtually, or in person, for an hour of yoga and meditative prayer open to anyone who wants to attend. You are starting a missional community if you gather young families together for a meal and hands-on activities that make Scripture come alive. You are starting a missional community when persons experiencing homelessness come together to set up food for a local food bank while praying for each other and talking about their faith.

Missional communities are popping up in auto shops, pubs, parks, and tattoo parlors. The pandemic of Covid-19 created virtual missional communities that meet in a Zoom room to talk about parables while eating pizza that they all ordered from a local restaurant. Missional communities are springing up by using the house party app where friends and friends of friends gather to play games and pray for situations they are facing during quarantine. Rev. Michael Beck's church in Florida launched "Living Room Church" to reach out to people looking for a virtual faith community when we were unable to meet in person due to the pandemic. It is a private Facebook group where people come together virtually to pray, meet in small groups and worship together. Within the first year, there were over 1,300 members of this online missional community, with more joining each day. Missional communities are new faces in new physical or digital spaces.

As your Expedition Team discerns the journey God is calling you to, consider whether a missional community is the right fit for you and/or your church. Perhaps, the Expedition Team may be called to start a network of missional communities! Any time "leaders of your faith community" is referenced herein, you could substitute a leader of the Expedition Team. Keep in mind, the community the Expedition Team is called to reach may or may not be the same community your church has or is called to reach. This is indeed part of the Expedition Team's discernment process as you journey into unchartered territory to reach new people.

You might be reading this and wondering why we need missional communities. Can't we just get more people to come to church instead of going to them at the dog park or in a Zoom room?

There are three main reasons why we need to take the missional community movement seriously.

1. The church is in decline.

Winfeld Bevins, in his recent book, *The Marks of a Movement,* notes that 80 to 85 percent of all churches in the United States have either stopped growing or are now in decline. An estimated three to four thousand churches close their doors each year and 660-700 thousand people are leaving the traditional church every year. The Pew Research Center has found that nearly one-third of young adults now say they have no religious affiliation."[3] In 2020, church membership in the United States dropped below 50% for the first time in Gallup's 80 years of reporting trends.[4]

2. We are not connecting with people outside of the church.

A Christianity Today article shares statistics that one in five non-Christians in North America doesn't know a Christian. And world-wide that number jumps to eight in ten.[5] A Barna study from 2019 reported that only two-thirds of Christians believe they have a responsibility to share their faith with others, which is a 25 percent drop from 1993.[6] Throughout the gospels, Jesus loves

[3] Bevins, Winfield, *Marks of a Movement,* Zondervan, 2019, page 23.

[4] https://news.gallup.com/poll/341963/church-membership-falls-below-majority-first-time.aspx

[5] https://www.christianitytoday.com/ct/2013/august-web-only/non-christians-who-dont-know-christians.html.

[6] https://www.barna.com/research/sharing-faith-increasingly-optional-christians.

spending time with people outside of the faith community. In Luke 7:34 Jesus is called a "glutton and drunkard" and a "friend of tax collectors and sinners" because he loved engaging people outside of the church. As I have traveled around the United States leading missional community trainings, I'm amazed at how many people don't know where to begin because they don't have any friends outside of the church. My brothers and sisters in Christ, let's be more like Jesus and connect with people outside of the church because we love them and long for them to find a meaningful relationship with Jesus!

3. Americans are experiencing widespread loneliness and a longing for meaningful connection.

In June of 2020, The University of Southern California reported that 1 in 3 Americans felt lonely at least once a week, which is an increase from 1 in 5 Americans prior to the outbreak of Covid-19. The highest rates of loneliness were reported in young adults aged 18-30.[7] If the church doesn't step in to create meaningful connections for lonely adults in our communities, they will find other outlets. The *On Being Impact Lab Report* entitled "How We Gather" shows that young adults finding spiritual connection at Crossfit, Soul Cycle, Artisan, or social justice groups are asking leaders of those communities to preside at weddings, hold funerals, or provide emotional and spiritual care. So younger generations are replacing faith-based communities with ones they have cultivated in their local gym or paint studio as they describe themselves as "spiritual but not religious."

How do missional communities help us address these three growing struggles in churches today?

There are many reasons why the church is in decline but one of them is the shift

---

[7] https://news.usc.edu/171124/anxiety-depression-covid-19-mental-distress-usc-survey.

we made in the 1800s to professionalize our clergy. Ken Nash is another contributor to the Greatest Expedition and he shared fascinating statistics at the "Navigate" Conference in 2019. Ken was impacted by the research of Roger Finke, a sociologist who stated that in 1776, when our nation was founded, there were 65 Methodist congregations, and approximately one in 50 Americans were a part of the Methodist Church.

By 1850, there were over 13,000 churches and one in three Americans felt a personal connection to the Methodist Church.[8] Today, less than four percent of religious Americans are affiliated with the United Methodist Church now. In other words, we have gone from 34 percent to four percent of Americans connecting to the United Methodist Church. What happened?

One major change is that we stopped empowering and equipping the laity to lead

---

[8] https://kevinmwatson.com/2009/06/17/the-explosive-growth-of-methodism-from-1776-to-1850

faith communities. Before 1850 Methodist congregations were primarily lay-led with a circuit pastor preaching every few weeks. After 1850, pastors spent time in pulpits instead of riding from circuit to circuit on horseback and so the laity didn't have the same responsibility to live as the "priesthood of all believers." Missional communities work best when they are lay-led with pastors serving as "circuit riders" who move from community to community, offering the sacraments and providing accountability and encouragement to these lay-led gatherings. Remember, John Evans was the first recorded convert to Methodism in America, and it was a lay couple that shared the good news with him. You can still visit the Strawbridge Shrine today in Maryland and learn more about Robert and Elizabeth Strawbridge and the inspiring work done by laity in early Methodism. Their legacy lives on in the laity who serve as the pioneers in these missional communities.

In Matthew 28:16-20, we read the powerful

words of the "Great Commission" but many
of us have a misunderstanding when it comes
to what we are being commissioned to do.
When we read Jesus' words to "Go and make
disciples of all nations," we think we are
being issued a command. But in the original
Greek language, the word "go" is not in
the imperative tense, it is not a command.
Another translation is, "**As you are going,**
make disciples of all nations." How much
larger would the kingdom of God be if we took
the Great Commission seriously? How many
more people would know the love and grace of
Jesus Christ if we embraced the notion that
wherever we go and whatever we do, we are
ALL called to make disciples?

Missional communities lean into that same
theological foundation as they challenge our
laity in the pews to go out into the community
and use their interests and gifts to make
disciples of Jesus Christ. Churches that
empower and equip their laity to go out and
start these missional communities experience

revitalization, not because the disciples who are made come and fill the virtual or physical pews each Sunday for worship, but because the faith of the laity comes alive as they have the profound experience of introducing people to Jesus and seeing their lives transformed.

I'll never forget the conversation I had with a woman I had met through mutual friends when we were at a playgroup for moms. She and I started talking about faith and after a few months she expressed a desire to be baptized. "So," she said, "if I want to take this faith thing seriously as I get ready for my baptism, maybe I should completely end the affairs I've been having and try to make things right with my husband. Do you think that's something God would want me to try and do?" We talked and prayed about her desire to practice faithfulness in her marriage as she prepared for a faithful walk with God. A year later, she and her husband shared their story of forgiveness and transformation with the entire faith community. It was a powerful testimony of discipleship and I was honored to be a part of her journey. When laity lead expeditions and starts missional communities, they can experience the mountain-top moment of witnessing disciples being made, and the joy and energy that brings can revitalize both the missional community and the established church that is praying for them as they serve.

Missional Communities also help us return to the important practice of offering relational and not just transactional outreach. Over the decades, the church has embraced the notion of "outreach" as a programmatic, transactional exchange. You come to the food pantry to get canned goods and then you leave. You come to the clothing locker for a new pair of pants and then go home. But missional communities offer a reminder that relational outreach can have both a physical and spiritual impact on those who are served.

When I was a church planter in Virginia Beach, we were partners with the local food bank and offered fresh meat, dairy, produce and bread every Wednesday to hundreds of families in the community. The majority of volunteers for that program were those who also came to receive the food, so they were either persons experiencing homelessness or living on the margins of society. Between twenty to thirty volunteers would show up every Wednesday around 1 pm to unload the truck of food and get things ready for the food bank program, which began around 5:30 pm. But they would have hours of time after unloading – and before 5:30 – so they would engage in a time of prayer and listen to sermons or talk about their faith. This time of discipleship was led by a layperson and this group of volunteers became a missional community. They were drawn together by their desire to access and offer food to their community, but a faith family was forged by their shared time together and the discipleship that was provided by an incredible layperson.

CHAPTER THREE

How Do I Start a Missional Community?

So, what does the process of starting a missional community look like?

I have spent some time with British Methodists comparing the ways that we equip and deploy the leaders of our missional communities and I developed this rhythm of starting new missional communities based on our mutual learning. The graphic on the following page illustrates this rhythm:

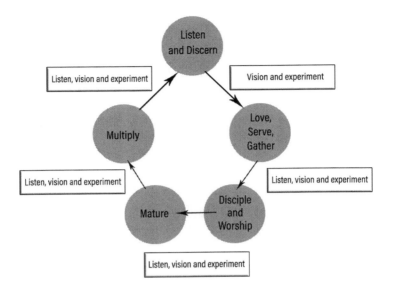

It's important to note before we dive into each step, that this is called a *rhythm* of starting a missional community. It's cyclical, not linear. It's a reminder that we can't see each of these steps as a box to check off and leave behind as we move to the next step. When you start a missional community, you are starting a movement that flows out of your church and into the community in an ongoing rhythm.

In the following chapters, we will dive deep into each step and explore how to move through the rhythm of missional communities.

CHAPTER FOUR

Rhythm 1:
Listen and Discern

This is the most important and hardest step for many church leaders. Why? Because we have all of this energy to reach new people, we think we know exactly how to do it, and exactly what our community needs. But if we do not stop first to listen and discern, nothing we create will be sustainable because it will be based on our thoughts and needs, not on the stories of those we are called to serve. In addition, we are often out of tune with what unchurched people need or desire since most churched people do not have many unchurched friends or family. We have lost touch with the very people we are called to reach. This is why the listen and discern rhythm is vitally important.

I was in the Peace Corps in Eastern Europe for two years. As a part of our training, we heard a story about a Peace Corps volunteer in Africa who was convinced that his role was to help his community build homes from more modern materials. The Peace Corps volunteer didn't like living in a home built from mud and sticks; he wanted his whole village to live in homes made from concrete or brick. So he spent two years showing his fellow villagers how to build a different dwelling by building one of his own and helping them to follow suit. When he returned to visit his village a year after his close of service, he noticed they were all living in homes made from mud and sticks again.

When he asked why, they said, "We didn't like your way, our homes were just fine." This Peace Corps volunteer gave two years of his life to create something entirely unsustainable because the origin of the idea did not come from those he was called to serve. So take time. Listen to your community. Here are some tips for what the listening rhythm should look like:

- Have a team of two or three people from your faith community commit to talking to a different person each week for at least three months. Encourage them to find change agents in the community like the school social worker, the head of the chamber of commerce, the bartender at the most popular bar in town, or a hospital worker in the local ER. Don't see your time with these community leaders as an interview, but more of a conversation. Find out where their heart and passion are, find out what they love most about their community and what worries them the most. Plan on spending no more than 45 minutes in each of these conversations.

- At the end of each conversation with a community leader, have your team summarize and document what they learned from the conversation in a shared spreadsheet that the whole team can see.

- After those three months, get together as a team and read over your summaries. Ask the following questions to guide the discernment process:

1. Whose voices were heard in these one on one conversations?

2. Whose voices were excluded from these conversations? What new information might those voices have contributed to the conversation?

3. What are the strengths of our community?

4. What are the challenges facing our community?

5. What is our community longing for?

6. Who could be our partners moving forward?

7. What is the best way to communicate with our community about what we've heard from them?

Once you have taken the intentional time to listen and discern how you can best serve your community, it's time to envision how you might be able to love, serve, and gather people in your community. What does this visioning look like? Have your missional community team write all of their ideas down and then ask yourself, which of these ideas will allow us to cultivate deeper relationships with people in our community? Now you are ready for the second rhythm of starting missional communities.

CHAPTER FIVE

Rhythm 2:
Love, Serve & Gather

This rhythm allows you to respond to everything you heard while you were listening to the stories of your neighbors as you spend time loving, serving and gathering with your community. There are four main principles to keep in mind while you are in this ongoing rhythm:

1. Christ's Radical Love to Your Neighbors.

If you love, serve, and gather with the main goal of growing your missional community numerically, you have missed the point; the true point here is engaging in Christ's radical love to your neighbors. So, don't show up at the community fair with flyers about your new missional community, show up with free hot dogs or balloon animals for the kids. Don't organize a food drive for the local food bank and turn it into an advertisement for your missional community as you host a revival service in the parking lot; focus on relationships and building up your partnerships in the community. In church planting, we train church planters to have strategic "hand-off events" where each gathering leads to another one that is bigger, more engaging to build your network, and helps you launch a large worship service.

Those who pioneer missional communities don't need "hand-off" events because the goal isn't 250 adults worshipping in a gym on a Sunday, it's about being scattered throughout the community helping people to follow Christ by modeling the radical love of Christ in what you do.

2. The Sixty-Forty Rule.

The next principle to keep in mind is the 60/40 rule. Most churches that start missional communities think of ways they can host or sponsor events at their church building or around the city. In this rhythm, you want to make sure that you are only hosting or sponsoring these opportunities to love, serve and gather 40 percent of the time. The other 60 percent of the time your missional community launch team needs to be the guest at these opportunities. This is a hard concept for a lot of churches to grasp because we are so good at scheduling and programming ministry that an approach where we receive the love and hospitality of others can seem foreign to us.

I like to think about the story of Jesus on the road to Emmaus in Luke 24:13-15. Jesus begins walking with these two men who do not recognize him. He asks them what they are discussing and they engage in a profound conversation about who Jesus really was. When the two men get to their final destination, Jesus continues on his journey until they urge him to stay and eat with them. After being their guest, he breaks the bread, and his true identity is revealed and their lives are forever changed. Jesus did not hand these men a flyer inviting them to the church Easter Egg Hunt. He didn't send them a Facebook invite to the next UMM pancake dinner. Jesus did not tell these men where to go or force himself into their home. He walked alongside them, asking questions and receiving their invitation to go deeper.

So, when you are in the love, serve and gather stage, try to ensure that at least 60 percent of the time you are responding to invitations from other leaders or non-profits to participate in service or gathering events that they are hosting. Offer to visit the local nursing home and bring flowers and cards to the residents when it is most convenient for them, not for you.

Go to the local pub and buy appetizers for the patrons inside when they have their busiest nights, not when you want to kick off your "Pub Theology" group. Attend the *meetup.com* book club Zoom call, not to invite everyone to your next Bible study but to learn, listen, and share as an invited guest to the event.

3. Balance Organic and Intentional.

In this rhythm, there will be opportunities to love, serve, and gather that come naturally and other opportunities that will be planned. If you linger in the parking lot to chat with other runners after you finish your workout, then it is an organic opportunity to gather. There might be other times where you organize an early morning "fun run" where a sponsor will donate money to the track team at the local high school for every mile you run together. Much like the 60/40 rule, make sure there is a balance between organic and intentional opportunities to love, serve and gather in your community.

4. Importance of Reflection.

The final principle to keep in mind is the importance of reflecting throughout this process. Continue to meet with your missional community launch team and ask them the following questions:

- With whom am I connecting as I love, serve and gather in my community?

- As I continue to listen to my community, am I hearing anything new?

- With whom could we partner as we move forward in our missional community?

- God was at work in this community long before we arrived. Where is God at work and how is God calling me to continue to love, serve and gather in this place?

You will also want to continue to reflect with those that you are meeting in the community as you love, serve and gather together. Have them share the ways that serving or making new friendships in the community has impacted their life. If they come from a faith tradition, they may use language from their upbringing to article what they are experiencing. So you might hear words like "transformation," "connection," or "servant" when they share about their experiences. But be open to those who are gathering with you that don't have "churchy" language and yet still want to communicate how these experiences are impacting them. Reflecting and continuing to listen are key steps to moving on towards the next rhythm of disciple and worship.

CHAPTER SIX

Rhythm 3:
Disciple and Worship

As your missional community launch team prepares to move from rhythm 2 of love, serve and gather to rhythm 3 of disciple and worship, it is important to take time to pray and plan out an intentional discipleship system and a philosophy of worship. Lay out your vision for what discipleship and worship will look like in this new missional community and why that model is important for you.

It can be tempting to read books on "best practices" for small groups, but when it comes to missional communities, it is important to take the context of your community into account. As the churched people who may be leading this missional community, we have to be careful that we do not impose our "traditional" customs of discipleship onto this missional community. Instead, those gathering in this new missional community need to have a strong influence on what discipleship looks like. What should your plan for this season look like? Here are guiding questions to answer before you begin this rhythm:

Step 1: Define Discipleship

Which of the following elements of discipleship are most important to us in this missional community?

- Studying Scripture

- Prayer

- Service to the community

- Telling others about our faith

- Obedience to God in our daily lives

- Developing a rule of life

- Demonstrating generosity in our time, talents, and resources

- Other _____

How will our discipleship system help us focus on the most important aspects of discipleship? It can be helpful to draw a visual example of what discipleship means to you. Whether you use the image of a mountain top, a plant that grows from a seed into a tree, or a pyramid, coming up with a visual example of what discipleship means can ensure everyone has a shared vision of what this will look like for your missional community.

Step 2: Lay out the Logistics

Now that you know what discipleship means to you and the elements of discipleship that matter most to your faith community, look at the practical side of discipleship and ask yourself:

• What kind of groups will meet?

Using your definition of discipleship, discern the best way to guide everyone in your missional community into a more intentional walk with Christ. You might have one group that studies a book on anti-racism and openly discusses the relationship between faith and actions. Other groups might prefer to have a time of prayer at the end of their soccer game or wine club and try out different types of prayer to learn more about how to communicate with God. You might have other groups that pick a book of the Bible and start reading it together to learn more about understanding God's word in both small groups and individual study.

• How many dscipleship groups will we have?

Expect a third to a half of your discipleship groups to have a rocky start and possibly not continue. So, the more groups you start, the better! Creating a fail-safe culture is crucial because this is an opportunity to innovate and learn as much from the groups that don't make it as those that do.

• Who will lead the groups?

If possible, have at least two or even three leaders for each of your missional communities. One person will take the lead with faith-related aspects of the group. The second person will be the host, welcome people warmly, and help build relationships and networks. The third person will be the communicator who sends out social media or text reminders to group members so they know where and when to gather.

• Who will train the discipleship leaders?

Take this time before the discipleship and worship stage of your missional community to train and equip the leaders on your team (if you haven't done so already). Spend time praying, learning, and engaging in fellowship together so you can empower and equip these pioneers to lean into their call for discipleship. This is a great way for the pastor to get involved and also offer spiritual gifts assessments or other tools to the discipleship leaders that can help them understand their strengths and grow in self-awareness. When I train small group leaders, I love to reference

Joel Comiskey's finding that the greatest indicator as to whether or not a small group will flourish isn't based on the theological knowledge of the small group leader, or on his/her/their personality but on the amount of time the leader spends in prayer.[9]

• Where will the groups meet?

Remember, meeting outside of the church gives you a presence with those whom you are called to serve. And with so many people becoming acclimated to meeting online due to Covid-19, remain open to the possibility of using Zoom or Google Meet or other online platforms as your virtual gathering space for discipleship.

• What age group or affinity group do we expect to reach first?

If you are starting a discipleship group for young families then you will need a plan

---

[9] Comiskey, Joel, *Lead: Guide a Small Group to Experience Christ*, CCS Publishing 2007

for discipleship for children. Will they learn alongside their parents or have a separate time to gather, study, and serve together? Does the place and time you have chosen for the group best meet the needs of those you are trying to reach?

When my church started a "Messy Church" missional community for young preschool families, we met for dinner on Friday night so that parents would not have to cook a meal at the end of the long work-week. A missional community that started out of a city softball league would meet after the games in a local pub for fellowship and discipleship. Be intentional about the group of people that you are most likely to gather and take their needs and preferences into account as you shape the discipleship options.

- Do we need funding for this?

Some missional communities leave a large tip for the service staff when they meet at their venue, but decide in advance questions of payment (i.e. who will pay for that?). If there is a book study for the missional community and someone doesn't have the finances to cover the cost, who will?

If childcare will be offered, what will the budget be for staffing and supply costs? When it comes to finances, recruiting the support and investment of the established church can be extremely helpful.

Strong communication and transparency are key. I met with a pioneer of a missional community who had received thousands of dollars of support each year for her dinner church. She thought she would continue to receive that money in perpetuity and was surprised when she learned that the anchor church no longer had the funding to support this ministry and it would end in six months. She had to scramble to find an alternate plan. Better communication would have benefited all parties involved.

Step 3: Determine benchmarks or goals for discipleship

This step begins by asking your launch team, "How will we know our discipleship system is effective?"

Missional communities that establish goals early on in the process are better equipped to make necessary changes to offer more transformative discipleship to those in their faith community. These do not and perhaps should not look like the discipleship goals that are used in the established church for end of year reporting. When it comes to missional communities and benchmarks, look for transformation and deepening of relationships. The goal is not to have large numbers attend your discipleship meetings but the quality of conversations and whether or not those involved in the missional community are sharing their experience with others. Social media makes it easier than ever to invite someone to attend your Saturday morning "prayer and paws" gathering at the dog park or the virtual "parables and pizza" group on Zoom. If the only ones talking about and inviting others to discipleship gatherings are the leaders of the groups, you might want to reevaluate your approach.

When my kids are excited about something, whether it be a good grade at school or a new hack they found on Minecraft, they want to tell me all about it and show it to me. When my friend Heather found out she was in remission from stage 4 breast cancer, she posted it on every social media platform available to her! In Jeremiah 20:9 the prophet says,

> But if I say,
> "I will not mention his word
>   or speak anymore in his name,"
> his word is in my heart like a fire,
>   a fire shut up in my bones.
> I am weary of holding it in;
>   indeed, I cannot.

When we get good news, we want to share it with others. Those engaged in discipleship in your missional community should be impacted by good news that they can't keep in, good news that they want to share with others.

——— Rhythm 3- Part 2: ——— Worship

It is also important at this stage to begin to develop a plan for worship. Keep in mind that those involved in your missional community may or may not ever participate in worship services offered by your established church.

Why? There are many possible reasons. Perhaps they grew up in a church with a traditional form of worship and were hurt by the people or principles of that church and so going back to a similar worship experience feels painful. Perhaps they attended a megachurch with contemporary worship but felt lost and never developed strong relationships and so they want every aspect of their faith journey to be deeply relational and held in a more intimate setting. Perhaps they have never attended church because they never had the opportunity. Perhaps they never attended church because of some horror stories they have heard about church.

Because the goal of a missional community is to reach those who have had no formal relationship with the church, the most likely reason is that they did not grow up attending church. So, the concept of getting dressed up to sit in a pew, sing from a hymnal, and pass an offering basket seems uncomfortable and foreign. So, as you develop a plan for what worship will look like in your missional community, it is important to begin by defining what worship means to those you are gathering, serving and discipling.

When I would travel around the United States and talk to churches about how to shape worship in missional communities, this was always one of the hardest lessons for them. They could not imagine calling something "worship" when it did not have all of the elements of worship in their Sunday morning, sanctuary-based service. But the outbreak of the Covid-19 pandemic forced churches to rethink how, when, and where worship could happen. Worship moved from a sanctuary to a living room and the elements of worship were adapted to an online space.

Use your same adaptive and innovative skills as you imagine what worship will look like in your faith community. Will it be an online service or podcast that your community can listen to throughout the week before you gather together for your time of discipleship? Will it be gathering in the dog park to share prayer requests and a brief meditation? Will it be singing in a local pub for your monthly "Beer and Hymns" worship service? Will it be practicing meditative yoga on Saturday mornings or gathering for a meal where people share stories from their own lives about how they have encountered forgiveness, grace, or healing? Will it be a part of the weekly discipleship meeting or will it be an additional weekly or monthly gathering?

Step 1: Define worship

As you define what worship will look like in your missional community, look at the following list to determine which elements you will incorporate into your worship experiences:

Prayer

Music

Corporate singing

Individual singing

Scripture Reading

Sermon/homily

Meditation

Offering

Communion/Love Feast10

Testimony

Discussion in group

---

10 The concept of breaking bread together as a gathered community can be found throughout the New Testament (Acts 2:42, 2:46, 20:7, 20:11, 27:35). John Wesley experienced a Love Feast when he spent time with Count Zinzindorff and the Moravians in 1727. It became a part of the Methodist movement and can be led by both clergy and laity. It typically includes a time of prayer, Scripture reading, testimony, and sharing a meal together. https://www.umcdiscipleship.org/resources/the-love-feast .

Children's Sermon
Time for Fellowship
Interactive Response [11]

It is also important to define how clergy will be involved in the worship experience. If missional communities are led by laity, then worship should be led by laity as well. So how and when will the pastor be invited into the worship experience? Will he or she come regularly to preside over sacraments when communion is celebrated, or will a layperson lead a "Love Feast" instead? If someone would like to be baptized, will the pastor invite the leader of the missional community to participate in the liturgy? Will the clergy person be invited to an annual "blessing of the animals" service in the dog park or to impose

---

[11] Many missional communities are adding in worship "stations" or ways for people to physically respond in worship. This can range from writing your sins on dissolvable paper and watching it disappear as you ask for God's forgiveness, or writing a promise to God on a rock and leaving it on the hiking trail as a reminder of your encounter with God or even molding and shaping objects out of playdough as you reflect on God shaping humanity out of dust in the Genesis account of creation.

ashes in the coffee shop or pub?

Step 2: Adapt

As you define and begin to shape worship in your missional community, leave room to adapt or innovate.

Don't be afraid to move one of your worship gatherings to a new location for a special service.

When I was a pastor in Virginia Beach, a missional community formed out of our city softball teams. On Mother's Day, we hosted a 9 am "Moms and Mimosa's" worship gathering at the pub that sponsored the softball team. The missional community gathered with members of the church and the community for a time of singing, communion, and fellowship. One of the softball players even had his son baptized in the service. It was the first time I had baptized a child in a bar. But it was a beautiful memory I will never forget as the church gathered in the community to celebrate a new life together!

Don't be afraid to change up the style or order of your worship service.

When shut-downs began across the United States in March of 2020 due to Covid, we initially saw a huge increase in the number of people watching an online Sunday morning worship service. Carey Nieuwhof wrote an article in April of 2020 where he cited Barna research that church attendance had gone up by 300 percent and over half of all churches in the United States. From small to megachurches, were experiencing growth.[12] For a few months we all celebrated until new data was released in July of 2020 that revealed one in three practicing Christians had stopped attending church, online, or in person.[13] While there could be many reasons for this decline, one reason was the lack of innovation or adaptation in online worship. Many churches

---

[12] https://careynieuwhof.com/half-of-all-churches-are-instantly-grow-ing-heres-why-and-heres-what-to-do.

[13] https://www.barna.com/research/new-sunday-morning-part-2.

found a rhythm that they liked for Sunday mornings and did not want to deviate from it. This led them into a rut rather than a rhythm of worship. So, add in times of silence, acts of service, or give your missional community a tangible way to carry worship with them into the following weeks. Think of ways to help worship come alive for your faith community as they continue to deepen their connection with God, others, and themselves.

Do talk about and practice generosity.

A common question when it comes to worship in missional communities is what the time of "offering" looks like. Again, be creative and adapt to your particular context, but do not exclude the practice of generosity. Generosity is foundational to living as followers of Jesus Christ and is an important act of worship! This does not mean that you need to pass around an offering basket when you gather. What could it look like? You could start a giving circle on social media that raises money for a cause that is connected to your missional community. You could collect supplies for a local school and pray over them in worship before dropping them off. You could all Venmo money to a single parent trying to make ends meet during difficult financial times. There is a myriad of opportunities to impact others with your generosity. So, find a way of giving and a place to give that resonates with your missional community. Talk about the impact on those who give and those who receive the gift.

Don't get into a numbers game.

Missional communities are not meant to become mega-churches. So, when it comes to benchmarks or goals for worship, look for **spiritual** rather than numerical growth. You are reaching people who have never been connected to a faith community before. Focus on what they are learning and how they are growing spiritually rather than the number of people who gather for worship. Matthew

18:20 says, "Where two or more are gathered in my name, there I am in the midst of them." So, take heart and know that when you gather, Christ is in your midst.

After you develop your discipleship and worship plans, launch them in your missional community and see what the Holy Spirit does! Continue to listen, vision, and experiment in this rhythm of discipling and worshipping. Celebrate what you are learning and how this missional community is learning to live as the body of Christ.

CHAPTER SEVEN

Rhythm 4: Mature

I remember the first time I tried to grow tomatoes. My husband and I had just moved into our home in Virginia Beach and I decided to start a garden. I don't have a green thumb and had never tried to grow my own produce before. But I was thrilled to purchase my first tomato plant. I put it in the soil, watered it, and came out day after day after day looking for signs of growth. When weeks passed and I still didn't have evidence of an actual, edible tomato on the plant, I wanted to start over and get one that would produce more quickly. My husband, an avid gardener, laughed and encouraged me to be patient. After more than a month I finally saw a little green tomato growing. My patience was further tested as

I waited for that little green tomato to ripen. When the tomato was finally ready to pick, I was elated and proudly cut it up for our salad that night at dinner. The months of waiting for that little tomato were frustrating, but that is part of the natural process of growth. There are some things you just can't rush. Not everything was made with a microwavable option and missional communities are the same way.

I was reminded of how frustrating it felt to wait for that tomato when I started a new faith community in Virginia Beach. Within a few months of launching, people were asking when we would start our youth program or begin fundraising for a building of our own. I happened to be pregnant at the time, so I reminded this newly formed faith community that we had to take our time to grow. We couldn't rush things, the same way that I couldn't rush my pregnancy. Over the next decade, our church plant moved from renting a theater to renting our own storefront space to eventually merging with an existing church and chartering as a congregation. I kept reminding the congregation that these things were all a process that could not and should not be rushed.

Even though missional communities are smaller and easier to adapt and multiple, it doesn't mean we should be adding a new community every week or every month before the first one is fully formed and mature. After launching the discipleship and worship plans, it is important to take time to learn and reflect and evaluate before moving to the multiplication stage. This rhythm of maturing could take weeks or months, but should not last more than a year. Here are the areas in your missional community where you want to look for maturity so that you are prepared for the rhythm of multiplication:

1. Spiritual maturity in members of the missional community

As time progresses, look at the faith

journey of those who have been regularly participating in your missional community. Are there signs of change? Has anyone from the community professed a newfound faith in Christ or shared openly about what they are searching for in their relationship with God? Have members of your missional community become more vulnerable in discussing what forgiveness or grace or generosity look like in their lives? Is healthy accountability being offered and received from those in the missional community? The main reason we start missional communities is to help those who are disconnected from God and the people of God start to cultivate those ties again. Is it happening in your context?

2. Maturity in leaders

The pastor of the church that is anchoring the missional community should be meeting at least monthly with the leader(s) of that group to encourage, support, pray, and equip the layperson. Common questions to cover during the regular meetings are:

- What are you celebrating right now in the life of the missional community?

- What concerns or growing areas do you see in the life of the missional community?

- What excites you when you think about the future of your missional community?

- How is your missional community continuing to listen, gather, serve and love the surrounding community?

- What are you learning about your discipleship and worship plans? Are they helping your community grow spiritually?

- What resources do you need to continue to lead your missional community and how can I help you with that process?

- What does your self-care look like right now?

- Can you identify one or more members of your missional community who might want to start one of their own? How are you training and equipping them to lead?

- When it comes to your physical health, are you able to continue leading the missional community right now?

- When it comes to your relational health with friends and family, how are things going?

- What is God teaching you right now?

- Is there a story of transformation from your missional community that I need to be sharing with the anchor church?

- How can I pray for you?

3. Maturity in future leaders

It is important for the pastor and the leader(s) of the missional community to pray, discern and discuss who else from the existing church or the new missional community might be ready for training as a future leader. When selecting someone to mentor for future leadership, you might want to consider the following:

- Spiritual maturity: Do they demonstrate the fruit of the spirit found in Galatians 5:22-23? How active is their prayer life? How open are they to accountability from those that they love and trust?

- Stage of life: Do they have or are they willing to create the time and space needed to lead a missional community?

- Relatability: While we all have different gifts, if you are leading a missional community you need to be able to strike up a conversation with someone without using "churchy" language or making that person feel pressured to give their life to Jesus in that very moment.

- Reliability: Because missional communities might only gather for an hour or two each week or month, it is important to have someone that you can rely on to show up on time and prepared. A pastor's worst nightmare is someone leading a dinner church who is scrambling at the last minute to throw something together for the meal and hasn't prepared any kind of Scripture or theme for the evening's discussion.

4. Maturity in relationship between the established church and the missional community

Missional communities have the greatest impact when they are led by laity but tethered to an existing church. The existing church can provide some resources to equip and fund these gatherings of new faces in new spaces. From administrative services to tangible resources like Bibles and books or pizza for "Pizza and Parables" night, the existing church can make it easier for the missional community to get going. They can also provide spiritual support, especially with regards to offering the sacraments in these missional communities, with the pastor being available to pray or counsel those who might have needs that the leader of the missional community is unable to fully meet.

In return, churches who support these missional communities usually experience revitalization. Not because these new Christians are coming to church every Sunday and filling out pledge cards each fall, but because lives are being transformed and new people are coming to know Jesus. The joy and excitement spread to the existing church as they celebrate the impact of this out-of-the-box faith community and the way that the kingdom of God is growing throughout their community.

How can this healthy relationship of the established church and missional community be fostered?

Spend time together

Outside of regular meetings between the pastor and missional community leader(s), it can be helpful to have one or two church leaders attend an occasional worship service or discipleship group at the missional community. There is a difference between hearing about what a missional community is and seeing it for yourself. Having one or two key church leaders participate in a gathering can help them understand and learn from these new faces in new spaces.

Do **not have** your entire church council regularly attend "Pub Theology." When you have more existing church members at a gathering than missional community members, it can change the feel of the event. It is no longer a "Pub Theology" session but has morphed into an off-site gathering of the Adult Sunday School class.

Serve together

Let's say your missional community meets each weekend to hike and pray. The missional community decides to sign-up for monthly highway cleanup to continue their emphasis on respecting God's creation. Invite the existing church to rotate clean-up days with you or send a few volunteers to help on your scheduled clean-up days. Serving together can help you feel connected in your mission to build the kingdom of God side by side.

When I was a pastor in Virginia Beach, I made regular visits to the local jail to visit a parishioner who was going to be behind bars for almost a year. Our visits were uplifting to both of us and she began sharing about her experiences with others in her block. One day she asked me if I wanted to meet a woman named "Muse" who grew up in the church and was longing for a spiritual connection. Muse became the leader of a missional community behind bars. She and I would meet regularly for accountability and encouragement. She would lead daily Bible studies and prayer times for those in their block who wanted to participate. On Christmas Eve they even shared in their version of communion by using juice and crackers from the canteen to represent the gift of Christ's love that gave them a taste of freedom behind bars.

One day Muse approached me with an opportunity for us to be in service together. A member of their missional community was nine months pregnant and was going to be released in a few days. Her mother was coming down from up north to bring her home, but finances were tight at home. They did not have money for the baby essentials that this newly released mother would need. The ladies from the church scrambled to purchase a new car seat and diapers and put together a care package of gently used items that they, as young mothers, had in abundance. When the woman was released and came to the church, she began crying when she saw the clothes, toys, bottles, crib, and books along with the car seat and diapers. A week later we all received a picture of the new baby with a beautiful thank you note from this mother trying to make a new life up north. The pictures and thank you notes continued for months. This formed a strong connection between the ongoing missional community in the local jail and the existing church.

Social Media

Both the church and the missional community should be utilizing at least one social media platform. By sharing or tagging each other in posts, you can help both groups learn more about each other as they access information about what each group is doing and the impact they are making in the lives of others.

5. Maturity in the commitment of missional community members.

One of the most exciting aspects of starting a missional community is giving ample time to see how people are changing and growing in their faith. I have a good friend who started a missional community in an urban city. He quickly developed a friendship with a self-proclaimed atheist who wanted nothing to do with God but liked the other guys in the group and wanted to spend time with them. As he continued showing up to their gatherings in the community, he began to ask questions about their beliefs and views on a variety of topics. Weeks and months went by until one day, the man exclaimed, "Shit! I think I'm a Christian." This man had no intention of being affiliated with a faith community or reconnecting to Christ, but the open and honest conversations in a non-churchy space led him to commit his life to Christ.

CHAPTER EIGHT

Rhythm 5: Multiplication

You might think that by the time you get to rhythm 5 of multiplication that it should just happen naturally. Unfortunately, that is not always the case. Intentionality is key in this final rhythm. Paul was the greatest multiplier that the Christian faith has ever known. He was strategic about training and equipping others so that the message could reach as many people as possible. In 2 Timothy 2:2 Paul tells Timothy, " And the things you have heard me say in the presence of many witnesses entrust to reliable people who will also be qualified to teach others." In church planting circles we talk about the multiplication to four generations that we see in this verse.

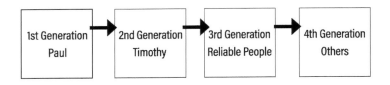

The instruction he gives to Timothy isn't about focusing on the number of people he reaches but on the importance of carrying on the message to future generations. Multiplication matters! Not because we want our end of year statistics on worship attendance to go through the roof, but because the message of God's love and grace offered to all humanity is a message that needs to be shared!

Paul never grew a mega-church. He was a leader of missional communities that became a network of growth throughout the Roman Empire. While he would go to the synagogue to try to share the good news of Jesus with the established religion of the day, more often than not you would find him in the center of town preaching to groups of philosophers (Acts 17:22-31) or tentmakers (Acts 18:2) or people he met while in prison (Acts 16:25-40). Paul would listen to the needs of his community and spend time gathering, discipling, and worshipping with these small groups of new believers before moving on to multiply and replicate the movement in other places. Paul had the essentials, ministry tools, and set off on a journey with his expedition team of Timothy or Silas or Barnabas. It was hard work, but deeply rewarding. Paul lived out a beautiful balance of hard, strategic work coupled with a deep dependence on the Holy Spirit to guide and direct his path.

So how do we move into this rhythm of multiplication?

The first step is to have done the important work of listening, visioning, and experimenting in between the rhythms of "mature" and "multiply." As you listen to the guidance of the Holy Spirit and develop a vision for when and how multiplication should happen, you will begin to see a plan take shape. It is also important to reflect on and celebrate the small ways that multiplication has been happening, even since the first rhythm of starting the new missional community.

- When you listen to a community leader share their hopes and dreams for the neighborhood and you are both so inspired that the leader introduces you to more leaders in the community, that is multiplication.

- When you are loving, serving, and gathering together in community and you invite your neighbor to come with you, that is multiplication.

- When you are worshipping with Beer and Hymns in the local pub and someone invites a friend to come with them, that is multiplication.

All of these acts of inviting and reaching out to others will help this rhythm feel more exciting and real to your missional community members. Remember, all healthy things grow. And in nature, they don't grow bigger and bigger: they reproduce. So don't focus on growing the largest missional community that your dog park has ever seen. Focus on growing the largest network of missional communities in dog parks that the world has ever seen!

What are the components of a multiplication plan for missional communities?

Start intentionally discipling and mentoring the leaders of your new missional communities.

Ralph Moore, who was a pastor in the Foursquare Church, multiplied his church plants and missional communities so intensely that over 2500 churches trace their origin to his decades in ministry. I was part of a Young Multipliers cohort where he came to share about his experience. He said that the process he used was simple. He would meet with 2-3 potential new leaders every week and ask them the same three questions:

- What did you hear God say to you this week through Sunday morning worship or your Bible study?

- Why did God say that to you?

- What are you going to do about it in the next 24 hours?

Moore's method was simple, but allowed his lay leaders to become attuned to listening for the voice of God, discerning how it should be applied to their lives, and responding with obedience. It is important to invest time, energy, and prayer in strengthening the relationships between the pastor or missional community leader and the new leaders. The Acts Network out of First Church in Williamsport, Pennsylvania is a network of missional communities led by Mitch Marcello. Five years ago, they started this initiative out of the established church. For the first six months, nothing happened and then things began to take off. Now they have 17 different missional communities. One meets on a field to play rugby. Others gather over a meal. Mitch is not clergy, he is laity. He is passionate about training and equipping others to start missional communities on a regular, ongoing basis.

Help your leaders understand their gifts and spheres of influence.

When your missional community leaders are self-aware of their own gifts and interests, they can be intentional about how and where they start missional communities.

I remember leading a discussion on missional communities with some amazing church leaders down south. One of the participants said, "I have been in a square dancing group for a few years. We meet every week. They've become like a family to me. They know I'm a Christian. I wonder if I could just reach out to that group to see if I can pray for them and maybe a missional community can form out of that dance group. What do you think?" "Yes!" was my enthusiastic reply. This woman knew the people she was trying to reach and had meaningful relationships and shared interests with the group. With support and mentoring from her pastor, she was able to reach out to her square dancing group and begin the initial stages of a missional community. The easiest place to start a missional community is a place that already feels like home to you. You don't have to send your leaders out to start from scratch. You can encourage them to see where God is already at work in their lives.

Be clear about what the purpose of a missional community is.

I cannot stress the importance of being clear. Missional communities exist to help people who do not have a relationship with God, or to help the church find a meaningful place to connect outside of the existing church body.

For whatever reason, there are people who will not feel comfortable or connected within the established church and this missional community will become their church home. You may never see them on a Sunday morning to count them in your average worship attendance, but they are a part of your church family.

But if multiplication of missional communities isn't about strong numerical growth in our churches, why should we care?

When I launched my church plant in 2010, 16 months after graduating from seminary, I used the "Lost" parables from Luke 15 as my first sermon series. These parables helped me understand, more than any other Scripture at the time, why it is so important to start new churches and new missional communities. Luke 15 begins with the Pharisees being critical of the way that Jesus allows tax collectors and sinners to learn in his presence. Jesus responds with a series of three parables.

In the parable of the lost sheep, the man

leaves the 99 sheep to find the one that was lost. He "joyfully" puts the lamb on his shoulders and invites his friends and family to rejoice with him because, as Jesus explains:

> *"...in the same way there will be more rejoicing in heaven over one sinner who repents than over ninety-nine righteous persons who do not need to repent."*

Let's be honest. A lot of churches with a rich and vibrant history do not have a bright future in store because there is not a lot of rejoicing going on. Exponential did research into established Protestant churches and found that six out of ten of them are in decline or have plateaued.[14] We aren't leaving the 99 to find the one.

When the woman loses one of her ten precious coins in the second parable, she looks frantically and doesn't stop until she has found the coin. Again, rejoicing ensues because:

---

[14] https://lifewayresearch.com/2019/03/06/small-struggling-congregations-fill-u-s-church-landscape

"...there is rejoicing in the presence of the angels of God over one sinner who repents."

How often do we try something new to reach people, whether it is a dinner church, support group for people in recovery, or a partnership with the local elementary school and when it doesn't bring new people pouring into the church right away, we stop trying? We stop looking. We focus more on **how** to keep our doors open rather than **why** to keep them open, **why** to reach new people. So, we don't find the lost coin. And we find that our joy is lost too.

And then we come to the third parable of the lost son. When this parable ends, the prodigal or wayward son is not the one who squandered his inheritance and lived a life of debauchery. At the end of the set of three "lost" parables, someone is still lost.

The rejoicing is not complete. You see, the older brother was too jealous of the celebration being held for his impulsive little brother and he couldn't join in the festivities.

This might be a parable, but it is also a reality in many of our churches.

Some of us have been in the church for so long that when we see someone new come through the doors who is full of joy and life after being transformed through the love of Jesus, we don't join in the celebration. We raise our eyebrows and complain that the music is too loud or there isn't enough food for the potluck or we aren't comfortable with a person *like that* in the house of the Lord. And we miss out on a great party, one that echoes to the heavens.

Earlier, I shared the story of the missional community that formed around a feeding program sponsored by my church plant. One of the most faithful volunteers in that program was a young woman, "Taylor," who found herself living on the street when she was only 15. By the time I met her, she was a few years older and pregnant with her first child. When the baby was born, "Taylor" brought her daughter with her to volunteer.

One particular day she asked me if her baby girl could be baptized at the church on Easter Sunday. I responded enthusiastically and we spent time discussing the meaning and importance of baptism. I asked "Taylor" why she wanted her daughter to be baptized on a Sunday morning when her connection with our church came through the missional community meetings we had on Wednesdays. "Taylor" said that she wanted the best for her little girl and Easter Sunday seemed like the best time to meet her full church family and let them share in the party. When that Easter Sunday came, we had a lot of first-time guests from the head of the incredible non-profit agency that works to get homeless teens off the street and some of her friends experiencing homelessness who wanted to be there to support her.

Indeed, there was a lot of rejoicing in our worship space that day. But I did overhear some grumbling at the end of the service from people who said, "Well, I guess we just let anybody come in off the street and join the church now" and "I've never seen that girl before. Why are we letting strangers join the church?"

This, my friends, is the situation you will find yourself in as you walk in the footsteps of Jesus, Paul, and countless others who went out to find the lost and bring them home with love and rejoicing. While most of the church, hopefully, will rejoice with you, there will be people who do not understand what you are doing. There will be people who will be threatened by all these new faces in *their* church. There will be people who start reaching out to the community with you, but when it is more difficult than they thought it would be, they stop the journey.

Take heart. You are doing hard and holy work, and it matters! Even if you have to leave the 99 to find the one, it will change the life of that one forever. All of heaven will rejoice with you. May you lean into this rhythm of starting new missional communities and find your own faith revitalized as you help people reconnect with God and each other!

What is The Greatest Expedition?

The Greatest Expedition is a congregational journey for churches, charges, or cooperative parishes led by a church Expedition Team of 8-12 brave pioneering leaders. The purpose of The Greatest Expedition is to provide an experience for Expedition Teams to explore their local context in new ways to develop new MAPS (ministry action plans) so you are more relevant and contextual to reach new people in your community. Updated tools and guides are provided for the church's Expedition Team. Yet, it is a "choose your own adventure" type of journey.

The tools and guides will be provided, but it is up to the church's Expedition Team to decide which tools are needed, which tools just need sharpening, which tools can stay in their backpack to use at a later time, what pathways to explore, and what pathways to pass.

the greatest
EXPEDITION

The Greatest Expedition provides a new lens and updated tools to help your Expedition Team explore and think about being the church in different ways. Will your Expedition Team need to clear the overgrown brush from a once known trail, but not recently traveled? Or will the Expedition Team need to cut a brand new trail with their new tools? Or perhaps, will the Team decide they need to move to a completely fresh terrain and begin breaking ground for something brand new in a foreign climate?

Registration is open and Expedition Teams are launching!

greatestexpedition.com

the greatest
EXPEDITION

These Books Now Available
as resources of
The Greatest Expedition

THE JOURNEY'S CALL

Returning to Our
Pioneer Roots

PHIL MAYNARD

the greatest
EXPEDITION

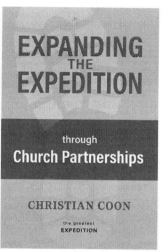

EXPANDING THE EXPEDITION

through
Church Partnerships

CHRISTIAN COON

the greatest
EXPEDITION

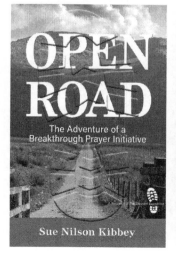

OPEN ROAD

The Adventure of a
Breakthrough Prayer Initiative

Sue Nilson Kibbey

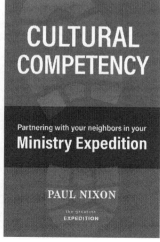

CULTURAL COMPETENCY

Partnering with your neighbors in your
Ministry Expedition

PAUL NIXON

the greatest
EXPEDITION

These Books Now Available
as resources of
The Greatest Expedition

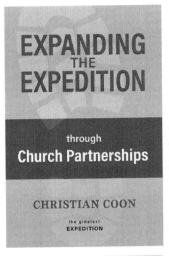

EXPANDING THE EXPEDITION

through **Church Partnerships**

CHRISTIAN COON

the greatest EXPEDITION

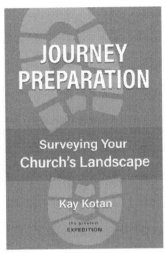

JOURNEY PREPARATION

Surveying Your Church's Landscape

Kay Kotan

the greatest EXPEDITION

the greatest EXPEDITION

A New Kind of **Venture Leader**

Olu Brown

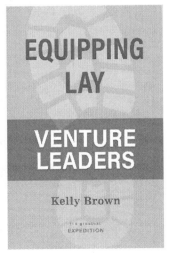

EQUIPPING LAY VENTURE LEADERS

Kelly Brown

the greatest EXPEDITION

marketsquarebooks.com

Quotes From Other Books
in The Greatest Expedition Series

The multi-site movement keeps the church centered on God's consistent call to go and make disciples for the transformation of the world while staying connected to one another in community.

Ken Nash
Multi-Site Ministry

Stay flexible even when it is not easy. Due to the stress and responsibility of ministry, we can become rigid, pessimistic and fail to see the opportunities in front of us. A mark of great leadership is flexibility, being able to make adjustments when necessary.

Olu Brown
New Kind of Venture Leader

But let me be clear, we will not be making the case that online relationships and connections are the same as in-person ones; we all know they are not. But we will be talking about why online connections are valuable, and there is nothing "virtual" or "almost" about them.

Nicole Reilley
Digital Ministry

Quotes From Other Books
in The Greatest Expedition Series

While we find struggling churches in different contexts, theological backgrounds, sizes, and cultures, declining congregations have one thing in common: There is a palpable lack of focus on what God desires.

Jaye Johnson
Missional Accountability

How you think of your church will determine not only your priorities, but also your energy investment and actions. It will define how you lead and to what extent you live into what the church of Jesus Christ is intended to be.

Sue Nilson Kibbey
Open Road

Any collaboration with local people is a good thing – but the best collaboration is spiritual. It is where we begin to pray together about the community, and the emerging ministry. In such a spiritual collaboration, amazing things begin to happen.

Paul Nixon
Cultural Competency

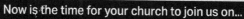

Made in the USA
Columbia, SC
12 July 2021

41744682R00054